Woman and Me

Becoming The Goddess

By Amy Jindra

This book is dedicated to women everywhere. May we all be so lucky to see the Divine in ourselves.

My Why

When I was four, I had a vivid vision that the moon was an ice cream shop.

The bright white color and craters sent chills down my little spine, a feeling I associated with ice cream. In one of my day-dreams, I went to the moon. Just like driving to an ice cream shop, but up. I ordered blue ice cream with sprinkles and sat inside the cold shop, staring out into dusty hills and valleys on the moon, the Earth a lovely marble in the sky.

I remember my desires, my emotions, my dreams, but I can't remember fear at this age. A four year old doesn't fear her feelings or her visions, that came later. There were other huge impressions stamped into me at four years old.

"Be a sweet little girl."

"Don't be so loud."

"That's unlady-like."

"Jehovah doesn't like this behavior."

My parents used the Lord to control my behavior. Being a little scientist, I always tested to see if what they said was true. In my mind, God's anger at me would cause a huge deluge or a plague, like in my favorite movie, Cecil B. DeMille's "The Ten Commandments."

Except, when I broke the rules--none of that happened. I just got whipped and called names.

I was a wild little creature. I didn't walk outside; I danced. I didn't say good morning; I sang it. I loved to test, touch, and spy. I felt things strongly and I was unable to hide those feelings, I couldn't shut my mouth. I made friends with anyone I talked to. I loved listening to people's stories. A fiery little being, I did not fit into the church or the world I was born into.

None of this aligned with the female role I was supposed to play: submissive, mild, and meek.

Nevertheless, I made the best out of going to the Kingdom Hall. I loved visiting with friends I'd charm with batted eyelashes and mischievous smiles. One was Brother Driscoll. He had curly silver hair, dark spots on his gnarled hands, and a pocket full of butterscotch or peppermint. He adored me. One Sunday, I galloped over to him and said, "Whatcha got?" with a big smile. He handed me a peppermint candy and gave me a wet kiss on my cheek. As I skipped back to our seats, happy as a lamb, my older brother Jon scowled at me. Irked by the fact that I had candy and he didn't, he snatched my candy away. He was much bigger and stronger than me, so I did what I could in defense: I bit him. I felt proud of my effort, not even caring about the lost candy.

My heart sank when I realized my mom had seen me. She was a sturdy woman with large hands and forest green eyes. She wrenched my little arm and yanked me toward the bathroom. I knew I was getting spanked and wriggled unsuccessfully to escape her death grip.

On the way there, she stopped to tell Ben Driscoll that I was a bad girl who had bitten my brother. At first he looked confused, then he looked disappointed. I couldn't look him in the eye. I could feel tears form in my eyes and my face got hot. I didn't want my friend to think I was bad.

I wasn't, was I?

My mother whipped me good. For the rest of the day, I sat completely frozen in my seat, still thinking about what happened. I can still see myself sitting there in my sky blue cotton dress, one of my favorites, with my stringy blonde hair, cut into a bob.

I was angry at my mother for not understanding, confused at myself for my emotion, and sad that my friend might think I was bad.

This idea of being the sweet little girl stayed with me into my adult life, and I couldn't shake her. It started off as me being a quieter child from then on, to being a straight A student, to living a life full of "shoulds" instead of passion.
I spent so much energy trying to prove to people that I wasn't bad.
I thought that if I catered to people and made them comfortable, then I would be safe and could earn love. A prison of expectations and a downward spiral of self hatred.
It also didn't help that I was never accepted as a Jehovah's Witness. I was disassociated publicly by the age of 13, for a crime I didn't understand.

It started when I was 12. He'd crawl into my window at night and whisper beautiful things. He promised he'd protect me and take me far away from my parents and my small town prison. Soon, he was holding me down and touching my body in ways that I loved and hated in the same moment.

I remember when I had to stand trial with the elders and one elderly man on the panel asked me if I had orgasmed. I had never heard of that before. I could still feel the disgust rack my body as a panel of old, white men described to me what an orgasm is so they could gauge my repentance for being sexually abused by an older member of the church.

I never quite landed in my body again. A sweet smile permanently plastered on my pale face.
This sweetness started to rot my soul.
When my mom died, I planned her funeral, cleaned out her house and still tried to run a business.

I showed up for meetings upbeat and and peppy, not showing any of my true feelings.

Outside of work, I cared for my husband, my dad, my friends, and everyone in my life.

"You are so strong," they said, as I developed stomach ulcers. Something was shifting in me, though. A wildness began to unfurl. She noticed how her husband tore her down when he felt stressed. How she took the wrap for mistakes made at work. How isolated she felt in every moment.

My mother's funeral was the worst day of my life. My father rambled family secrets to anyone who would listen, my husband wandered awkwardly around the room ignoring me, and the speaker questioned whether my mother was really anointed and going to heaven as she believed. And I had to go to a Kingdom Hall again. I never imagined under any circumstances coming back here. The thought of it kept me up late at night in a cold sweat.

I tried to be nice, but I couldn't. I couldn't keep the anger and bitterness from my voice, so I turned to alcohol for help.

After a family dinner, where I drank myself silly, I met up with friends. Nghia, my husband, couldn't tolerate my emotional self anymore and dropped me off.

I continued to drink late into the night and wandered off alone down a cobblestoned road to snag a cigarette. Except my heel caught, and I fell. My phone went flying, and I laid in the street, too drunk to move. I laid there crying and bleeding for what felt like an hour.

An angel finally came in the form of a sweet little college girl and her friends. They helped me up, tried to find my friends and eventually called my husband for me. Nghia was so angry. He wouldn't speak to me on the car ride home. The next day, he chastised me for being reckless and told me he would not replace my lost phone.

A week later, miserable and isolated, I mentioned Nghia's words to my friend Jenny, who exclaimed, "You kidding me? Amy, you're an adult with a bank account. BUY A PHONE." In that moment, something clicked. The power my husband held over me wasn't real. I was accepting this invisible cage.

This was the end of my marriage, and of the Amy who cowered and hid her true feelings. The Amy of my childhood began to reemerge. She began to test, to touch, to spy. She was free.

Freedom starts with honesty. Ugly, scary honesty.

I spent years pretending to be the perfect daughter, the perfect wife, and the perfect Christian, not showing my feelings, staying silent in the face of emotional abuse and sexual violence.

When I finally got honest with myself, I could no longer perform. My soul was too wild, too loud. Despite my anxiety and fear, I travelled the world, I moved to New York City by myself, and I decided to commit to being more of myself each day.

Through ancient tools and practices like tantra, meditation, prayer, caring for my body and setting healthy boundaries with people in my life, I began to learn who I truly am.

I have to choose to let God be what's in front of me and around me -- not the tyrannical old man I was taught to fear. Each day I am able to be more honest, uncover the source of my fears and guilt, and return them to their source. It's not easy, but I choose real instead of easy this time.

I'm ready to live in a world with a freedom of pure expression and emotion.
These poems have been a huge part of my healing and

reflection of myself as a woman.

I'm ready to live in a world with a freedom of pure expression and emotion.

I am ready to be a woman in all her divinity.

Surrender– The sexiest word I know.

Woman and Me by Amy Jindra 2018

www.womanandme.com

Divine

You can have everything you desire, it's here.
You just have to let go. Let go of fear, control, shame,
obsession and insecurity.

Trust that you are important.

Trust that you are necessary.

Your clients are waiting for you.

Your prosperity is here. Stop clenching and fearing
money, my dear. Stop making up worst case scenarios.
Stop expecting struggle.

Paths are already lined up for you. Each step you take
forward and say yes to your purpose, more will be revealed to you.

You are a miracle. You cause miracles everywhere you
go. You bring good fortune with you. You bring prosperity. Shine your light upon yourself.

Love is also coming for you. Don't be afraid of it. You
can have prosperity and love. In fact, one requires the
other. Just allow. Keep showing up and stay open.

Your life is glamorous. You are glamorous.

Let it be easy. You are so supported.

Tantric

Today I made love to myself.

I saw my beauty.

I felt the softness of my skin.

I felt my breasts and became hypnotized by the sound
of my own breath.

I was soothed by the rocking of my hips.

Comforted by my warming nectar.

There was no beginning or end.

No Judgement.

Just a beautiful goddess feeling.

Truly feeling. Creating. Connecting. Living.

Waiting

Waiting wasn't easy.

I touched my waist as you would.

I spoke to your side of the bed.

I cleared out your side of the closet.

Hoping you didn't mind I painted the hallway pink.

I feel you so close.

Your strength, your fire.

I feel your need to act and help.

Your faith pushes me forward to jump into my dreams.

When I land, I know you aren't going to side track me.

You enhance my dreams, my desires.

You magnify and multiply.

Your gifts fit beside mine.

Your hands fit around mine.

Your heart fits in mine.

Into The Sky

I'm ready to let my suitcase of mold, excrement, bricks and pain go.

At first I didn't know where to put it.

The victim in me didn't want to burden the Earth or the sidewalk with it.

I have to hold onto it. It's heavy, it's sad. It's mine.

Who would I be without my baggage?

My arms wouldn't have anything to hold.

My muscles would grow weak without this heavy load.

Walking in my subconscious one day, a blast of wind hit my face, caused my balance to tip and my suitcase nearly slipped from my grasp.

Another swirl of warm air danced around me and I clutched my heavy bag to my trembling body.

I can't lose my bag.

It's all I know. It's familiar. It's mine.

The currents kept coming. My hair flying, my face clenched.

The wind felt so good.

I wanted to dance in it. Let it take my arms and sway my body.

My eyes closed in imagination.

Before I could register what happened, my bag was lifted.

The further it flew away, the less I reached for it.

A moment of panic came when I opened my eyes.

It's gone.

My hate, my worries, my shame and guilt.

Before I could completely break down in my

identity crisis,

the wind came back.

Warm, gentle, blissful.

And in this moment, I found everything.

Sweet Girl

Relax, sweet girl.

Your dreams aren't too big.

Your visions aren't too vivid.

There is a soul looking for you.

He's restless and longing. Wanting a soul connection in vivid green.

His fire is bright and consuming, rarely is he able to unleash it.

This match was before your birth,

perhaps a continuity of another life.

The fears you have match his strengths,

Your softness is a balm to his burns.

Your hearts will recognize each other.

They can't miss.

There's a field surrounding you that calls to him.

Let him pursue, do not force.

Sweet girl, he's already here.

Me Too

It lives in me.

The fear that shines in your eye.

The guilt in my chest.

The beauty of your sliver moon.

The universe lives in me.

The joy, my failures.

Healing and change.

When the sky grays and weeps, I too

am thunderous.

You reflect me and I, you.

A giant tree with curvaceous leaves,

a single line of ants.

A delicate thread of silk.

I am good, I am bad, I am nothing.

Except everything lives in me.

I am Egyptian.

I am wolfish.

I am as proud as a peacock.

My soft spots are a siren's song

to your demons.

But I must say, I relish your attempts

to knock me down.

My strength is in my softness.

My vulnerability is my greatest success.

Venus

I am in heaven.

A sea of my favorite colors

splashing against ancient rocks

that warm and grate my skin.

The sun lifts my face and softens the wind.

I am not alone.

I speak to myself, to her, to us.

There is no hermit by the sea.

There's too much life to be alone.

There were battles, great loves,

death, joy, rebirth.

I feel it all lying on this rock.

Understanding how immense and

fleeting this moment truly is.

I'll stay as long as she does.

Pardon Me

Pardon me, you left your fear in my arms.

Getting dressed, I felt an extra layer.

The stock market, education reformation,

stifling aristocracy.

When we embraced, I was soothed by your warmth.
Your skin, gritty and acidic, made mine seem extra special and tender.

Your solid chest gave a stillness I hadn't seen.

Your growling timber, reminding me to hush and enjoy the stillness.

I left and these sensations wafted away, worry did not.

It wasn't until midday, as I processed and categorized my emotions, did I realize someone else was there.

You see I am used to the fears of a woman.

Not always feeling safe, not being seen or considered.

Yet today I took on a new darkness that didn't belong to me.

Telling me to panic. Asking me to rage and gnash and bloody my knees.

Putting blame on the ones that are different.

Itching to share these sentiments, because commiserat-
ing may give me some soothe.

Pardon me, you left your fears in my arms

and they're yelling over mine.

Picasso

Picasso said that Art and Sex are the same thing.

I realize this every time you touch me.

It changes me, it heals me.

When we touch, all emotions move through my veins, nerves and cells.

You're an alchemist.

Your love has transformed me.

The miracle of meeting you reminds me that I am here at the right place, at the right time for a big, big purpose.

When we breathe together, I lose track of whose body is mine. The electricity of your pleasure flows through me.

I orgasm throughout my entire body. Waves of bliss blast to all my channels. Healing, changing, repairing.

I don't have to be polished and manicured.

I don't have to be polite or sexy.

Our movements are instinctual.

Our love is primal and transcendent.

I couldn't worry about the way I looked if I wanted to. I no longer exist.

Just pure, blinding light mixed with shadows from my deep, red fire.

I could fill a museum with paintings of our passion.

I would need a second building for the sculpture of our connection.

Sacred

My beloved, come inside.

I secretly love when you make me wait.

Sneaky smiles reveal your wicked fire.

Let me burn, for now.

I writhe and I scheme.

Your hesitation is thrilling,

but my temper swirls.

On my golden platform, I tense.

Not knowing your timing,

guessing at your intentions.

Lick me with your vibrant light,

heat me with your sharp gaze.

Stay now till tomorrow.

Overwhelm me and let me cry.

Then brace yourself for my flood.

I surrender. I fall with no crash.

Your lips whispering into my hair keeps me sane.

A thousand years flashed between my eyes.

Stay inside, beloved. Please.

Wicked

In my power I am deep and fiery.

My presence is felt, my gaze is laser sharp.

The smile on my face is loving and easy, but I see every-thing.

I not only see it, I feel it. I feel what is going on in my bones.

I used to hide away my power, lessen it, ignore it.

Now something in me giggles when I see someone afraid of me.

For I am a mirror, and you are afraid of yourself.

Wild Woman

I want to become the fire.

I want to sway my hips, look people deep in the soul and always keep my fire.

I want to be too much.

Shake the furniture.

I want to question everything and learn as much as I can.

I want transformation and experimentation.

I want to be ripe and gushing.

I want transcendence.

I want to transform anything I touch.

I move with ease and intention.

I wake up everyday to love and beauty.

I am unapologetic.

I am wild

I am fire.

Alien

I'm living bliss.

Memories of last night flash through my mind.

Candles, sweat, writhing primal bodies.

No end and no beginning.

Hours of eye open, microcosmic orbit, meditative,

connected sex.

And even sweeter, this morning.

As he kissed my neck and traced my freckles,

"Did you know you have constellations on your back?".

Lilith

Today is such a gift.

I'm going to show up for it even though I'm not ready.

Even though I'm not worthy.

Even though I'm not strong enough.

Today is mine and I will show up anyway.

Gwen

Love is a beautiful thing. I am not afraid
of it.

I am intense.

I am open, clear and emotional.

I don't play games.

I can't play anything cool.

I am in or out.

I ask for what I need.

I tell you when I am upset.

I will not convince you to be with me.

I am intentional.

Awakening

Sunlight and cotton

Coffee with sex

Oil or acrylic

As long as it's New York.

Neroli

Watch.

Watch Grace flow through your steps.

Your body forgot.

Listen.

Listen to the music of your breath.

It's magic.

Taste your own lips.

Salty and wild. They are for you.

Caress your neck.

Trace your fingers across your ribs.

So much life flows through you.

Your smell is floral and fragrant.

I can't wait for you to sweat.

It's okay to forget,

But I'm so glad you're home.

The Savage

You told me you were a savage.

I felt it.

You opened to me in a frantic way.

We danced on a stage

then under the stars.

We sat still together and breathed.

You're overwhelming and wild, desperate to be in control and adored.

I'm not sure if I miss you

or the possibility of us changing the world.

So much power, so much pain.

We are both God.

I'm your melody

You're my muse.

A flash of fear and wild desire.

I hope you call

And if you don't.

I got to touch something a little too hot.

Hudson

My angels are close today,

not even whispering.

People don't understand you. So what.

Sometimes you're alone– That's okay.

Your darkness is suffocating– Learn to roar.

Just stop fighting.

Return to yourself.

Change is here, allow it.

Be easy.

Swamped

Rage is beautiful, I'm learning.

Grief, too.

Tears are my jewels.

Sobs are really earthquakes, dislodging old stories.

Screams and growls are cleansing breaths.

It's not about being proper, it's about being both– human and divine.

Our pain may not have a purpose, but our rage and grief do.

Let it rise, let it turn you on.

If you push it down,

when you push it down,

It eats your joy, your bliss, your ease.

Find the power in these emotions.

Not ugly, not weak.

Rage and grief complete you.

Missing Mama

I know you feel reckless, Wild Girl.

You left Texas in a blaze.

The cowboys are relieved and your girls are still crying by the fire.

You're a fighter and a liar, but we miss you just the same.

The world seems too big with you so far.

Walking on water in your high heeled boots.

Come home, Wild Girl.

Remember your roots.

Divine

I wasn't ready for you.

You are a king and I was a witch.

You are pure calm and integrity, looking for the best for your following and your legacy.

I was chasing love and manipulating with my words and candles.

I move into Queen and Divine Healer.

I give up my projections, obsessions and control.

I could not love you unconditionally until I accepted my divinity.

As I relax into my power, I allow you to take the lead.

Wounded

I hate you a little bit.

You bring out a hidden self that has never seen the light.

A voice inside that wants to cling to you. Make you obsessed with me.

The same voice that tells me I'm wrong, difficult,

unworthy, incapable.

I wanted to make myself important with your face.

I wanted to feel successful with your body.

I wanted safety in your fame and wealth.

I thought I could find home if you held me long enough.

If I convinced you of how broken you are and how much you need me, maybe I could relax a little.

The way I pick you apart really isn't about you.

I have a sick past.

Men put me on a pedestal and grow more and more gray each day, and so do I.

I used to play the role of mother and superman.

Giving them a false love that felt warm, but was hurtful and destructive.

You see, I'd never felt love.

Couldn't recognize it. To be honest, I pushed it away most of my life.

Not understanding that love is what thaws me.

Unlocks me.

Heals me.

Love doesn't feed my darkness. So I thought it wasn't for me.

Until I realized that I am love.

As I return to myself, I am slaying my demons.

My patterns, my manipulations. My tantrums.

My projections.

I can't promise you tomorrow. But today.

Today I accept you fully.

As I completely love and accept myself.

I Am A Drummer

I am a drummer.

I beat a rhythm that used to keep me up at night.

A pulsing of Gaia, safety, dirty wild and beautiful.

I take the pain of isolation, and a strumming of my
hands against leather-

And I let it cry out.

I feel the tension of failure, with every bang my chest
hangs looser.

He didn't call, I thrummed a rhythm so sweet, that my
tears ran with joy.

I am a drummer.

The pulse of a melody with no words.

A Million Women

I don't march in anger.

I came for love and to remove all barriers to love.

My prayer is that it's easy.

My prayer is that it's joyful.

Don't let it stop with this march on this day.

Join me.

Glimpses

I see you.

Even when you have your guard up, your soul talks to me.

She's beautiful, your soul.

She has grand plans and loves endlessly.

She is power and prestige and famous.

When I see you reading a room, giving people glimpses of yourself, my soul hurts.

I am warmed when your spirit winks at mine.

You see, you can have sacred. Or you can have perfect.

Your mess is sacred, my love.

Embrace it, share it, roll around in it.

Your mess is what changes people.

Changing the world feels really big, but it's not.

Your soul has already begun.

Cancer Moon

A portal is open this evening.

Take my greed.

Take my lies.

Take my corruption and laziness.

Take the whiny child that is afraid to face herself.

Take the indulgent whore that values her body as a transaction. She doesn't understand her divinity.

Take the people pleaser, the good girl.

She rots my teeth.

She is decaying and already dead.

Numbness is her only solace.

Take the control freak, the nerd. Her depth is limited. Her love is stale and ruled.

Leave me with the Goddess, the Lioness, the Warrioress, my Queen.

Her prayers are commands.

Her presence is alchemical.

Her love is deadly, for when she loves you-

nothing unreal lasts.

Nurse

When you can no longer feel,

have my warmth.

When you can no longer breathe, use my lungs.

I am not a person. I am not myself.

I am a healer.

Sound Bath

Deep in my subconscious

there lived a story.

Every night as I slept, this story would leak.

Spread through my skull,

drip down my spine

and curl around my organs.

A story so dark and scary that it was ignored.

A silent thief.

For this story stole my joy, my health, my happiness.

April

Have I always been beautiful?

Because I am feeling it for the first time.

Has my walk changed?

People turn when I stomp past.

My body is so strong.

Such an incredible vehicle carrying me through this life.

When I catch my eyes in a reflection, it's impossible to look away.

They're deep, fiery,

A vibration of natural chaos.

When I sing, I hear the earth in my voice.

When I dance, snakes of pleasure bend and twist, charming any rhythm.

Why is it now that I notice?

When no one is there to tell me.

When I stopped the cycle of seeking.

British Buddha

I wish I could write.

The lighting is perfect, it feels like Europe.

I want to explain how good your jaw smells,

how long your legs are.

Every time I grasp for words,

they vanish.

A cloud of dusty chalk,

erased from my brow.

So instead,

I'll lie in your arms,

smiling into my pillow.

Wishing one day I'll write a poem about this moment.

Psalm

After every laugh, you pause.

Savoring the sound.

Your life has been full of pain, but you're ready to laugh more.

Your heart has been shredded, and yet, you love completely.

You're not a savage at all, they just don't understand you.

You're wild to the unopened soul.

To me, you are the order of the universe.

You fight, you bleed, you observe, you stand back up.

You guard, block, wrap and warm.

I'm sorry if I never told you– I think you're beautiful.

I remember asking God to end my feelings for you.

To break our ties.

It was cold, my poetry shallow and weak.

The pain of my cowardice slipped through the gaps in my teeth.

My smile, never real.

My soul wasn't done loving you.

Perhaps punishment for a past life.

I remember you didn't love me either.

Sex was a battle of power and deceit.

We deserved each other in those brutal moments.

And today I picture you as I am warmed by spring.

You're the last I know of love with a man.

So I use that as an anchor into love.

You or something better.

Did I fail some test?

It was as if I started to fall, so I clenched and held my breath. I did end up falling, but when I opened my eyes only an outline of you remained.

Burned into my eyelids.

I can barely smell you anymore.

Art

Everyday I choose art.

To me, art is such a perfect example of love.

Sparked. Given. Shared.

It looks different for every artist,

then reinterpreted by each observer.

Mediums, vehicles, colors, lighting– all different.

We have our preferences.

Then something out of our norm comes along and cracks us open to new possibilities.

My Shiva

My heart already belongs to someone.

I don't know who he is, but he's important.

And worth waiting for.

He pulls me in with his gaze.

Keeps me there with his warmth.

A man of charisma, power, strength.

I can only pretend I know his voice.

Can only imagine what his smell does to me.

I melt in his arms.

I ignite in his presence.

God help me to open to him.

To allow. To fully love.

We are wild together.

Public is a place to dance around our magnetic pull.

Letting the tension build.

We don't kiss or touch.

Because we know it would explode.

We stand too close. Breathe too deep and dance too sexy.

He's there to catch me.

Because every time I fall.

His arms are grounding. His love is loud and solid.

A presence that can reach me through space and time.

I feel him now, my nipples are hard.

He's laughing.

He has the sexiest laugh.

My ears are growing warm.

A sensation I haven't encountered before.

I want to stay open to the love meant for me, but I pray
for a tall, dark, fit man.

A gift to my senses. A fire to my chest.

A constant tingling between my legs.

There is no dominating him, only loving him.

A Shiva. A man of healing.

He sees everything in me and still wants me close.

I pray for the eyes to see him.

The patience to hold room for him.

I trust the universe.

I trust love.

I trust that my desires are divine.

I Let You Go

I let you go.

Did you let me go?

I burned a piece of paper with your name on it.

I miss the way you laugh.

I asked God to cut the cord.

Your chest is so warm.

Severing our connection.

I felt safe and quiet.

I remember you didn't kiss me. It kind of broke my heart.

I would have waited

I just can't be an after thought.

Moments of bliss.

Shadows of disappointment and obsession.

My love is too big, too hard

Too Scared.

City Girl

I couldn't sit still.

I walked in the snow,

sliding in my high heeled boots.

I wonder what my lover's doing.

I walk into a burger place,

turns out to be a bar.

The glasses are green.

St. Patrick's Day.

March 16th is always hard for me.

Out Of Body

Baby, you're it for me.

The woman that can't stop smiling,

She's a good listener.

When you laugh and in turn everyone laughs with you.

You trust, knowing you trust yourself.

You love, knowing the rewards.

You may be too much, but you don't hold back.

The lonely feel seen.

The rain sounds tempting.

The glow doesn't require follow up.

It. You. We.

Jezebel

The veil is lifted.

My inflated ego, dark and thoughtless.

A black cloud leaking through my punctured chest.

Releasing my false power,

my hunger to seduce.

My witchy compulsions.

The intoxication of meaning and purpose,

Woven with immaturity of lack.

As the acrid cloud dissipates,

I tremble in gratitude.

It is not me at all.

I am a being of light.

The veil is lifted.

Temple On A Hill

There's a temple on a hill.

I walk slowly on this dirt road,

my body being pulled slowly.

One foot gliding in front of the other.

Kissing the earth.

An ancient drumming matches my heartbeat.

I've been here before.

A crowd of servants appear behind me.

Cleaning the cobwebs,

laying silks and cushions in my path.

I realize I'm naked as I ascend the steps to my holy place.

She's here.

Behind me I feel her power, a true Queen:

"You've returned."

"I've hit rock bottom. I can't keep going."

"You have endless treasures in this earth. Your power is still burning, the temple just deserted.

You're home now. Breathe, Sister."

For the first time in centuries,

my breath filled my belly.

Hardened my nipples,

brightened my eyes.

A hiss tickles my lips and a grin begins to stretch.

My golden crown, gleaming with divine responsibility.

Karma

Last person on the plane,

running through the airport barefoot,

shamelessly dreaming of sex.

She remembers the smell of his jaw,

the texture of his hands,

the sound the moment he surrendered.

The primal joy protects her from the chaos sitting beside her.

A dip into darkness.

He says she brings out his devil.

She feels like the universe on his chest.

How can an experience so quick still tear through her body?

They both don't know why.

She loves him and hates him.

She loves the way he touches her,

with his voice and his feet.

There's medicine in their touch.

Her soul longs for him,

not knowing if he's a lesson or a present.

Something left last night.

That fear of losing her mind.

He revealed he'd lost his.

It's not a one-sided affair.

And it took the fear away.

The fear of rejection, being a bother, obsession and missed opportunity.

He feels it too.

Mine

Have you ever been worshipped?

Not because of how you look or who you are,

but simply because you're a man?

Your heart beat, a pulse of your throne room.

Be adorned and loved

because you observe this world and hold a foundation
for my creation.

Let your body be my altar.

Stay unafraid of human attachment.

I see the universe on your skin.

As I kiss, lick, touch and caress-

I am praying through you.

Your pleasure is my connection to the infinite.

Remove you and I.

Let my soul penetrate yours.

My mouth is greedy,

but my intentions are pure.

Lonely Planet

You say when I write about you,

You become a planet in my solar system.

This made me deeply sad.

A planet.

Rotating, revolving.

Pushed and pulled, but never touching.

Not connecting. No joining.

I would burn you up.

We would crumble.

I try not to write about you, my bold planet.

Yet we are not joining on this plane either.

I'm burning alive.

What have you written about me?

Lioness

I miss my illusion.

The glimpse of my relationship that never came.

A love so big and wild.

I bare my teeth and growl, showing you my heart.

Unable to sleep because there's never enough time with you.

Never minimizing or hiding my magic, my darkness or my past.

Your skin calls to mine.

Frustrated tears burn my eyes until I lay my heart on yours.

You didn't want to get burned up.

A blazing fist, punching through your belly, up your spine.

I'm not sorry. I changed you.

You also changed me.

An oracle told me not to judge you.

That I'd be like organic fruit. So good for you. Refreshing. Healthy.

And you.

You got me dreaming.

I don't know what form my Shiva's in.

But I feel him and I honor him.

Love Story

It's always a love story.

Feel brand new today because you want to–

not because it makes sense.

Remember that incredible lover that you would drop everything for and run to, just to have an hour in their arms?

Take that feeling, and make it about you.

Run back home to yourself.

Get excited to touch your own skin and connect with your breath.

Hold a secret just for you.

Let it shine through your eyes and your crooked smile.

Let that secret move your hips in a new way, push your chest out.

Your love story just got juicier.

I look back on the darkest times in my life

and realize–

How romantic.

The universe challenged me to go deeper.

To feel so deep that I understand how important the rain is.

To love so hard that heartbreak is worth every memory.

To realize there is no broken, just faceted.

A New Way

That is not your real name,

but I don't know what to call you.

I am not your teacher, I am here to open you.

I see your innocence.

I see your light and your dark.

I honor them both,

knowing they are perfect.

You were not born a child.

Your sweet soul came into a world of isolation and

sadness.

Look at you.

Your struggle for good.

Fighting.

Always fighting.

Fighting your pleasure,

your purpose, your softness.

Relax into me.

Into this safe place.

Let God meet you, let it feel good.

Fighting your soul.

Fighting your heart.

Fighting me.

I see you.

Lay down your muscle.

Instead of hitting a wall and trying to find release against it, let them melt.

Let your power soften.

Trust the people you try to possess. Trust yourself.

Feel the fire in your body, but harness it.

Keep it in your belly where it has value.

Accept your lies.

Accept your ability to manipulate and possess.

Do not judge what the Divine has created.

Even at rock bottom, God made those rocks.

I am not your great love or your friend.

I am a mirror, illuminating the wounds you refuse to heal.

The reminder that we all have our roles in this movie of life.

Sometimes you're the hero, you're also the villain.

Above all, stop lying.

To the world. To me. To yourself.

Start to see the sacred in your darkness and let it go.

Finding abundance and wealth by the way of pleasure and joy.

I see you.

Your ability to see beauty in men and women.

The instinct to act unapologetically.

Your power, your tricks.

Your connection to the divine and your impulse to cut the cord.

It's time.

The past doesn't exist.

It's not real.

Lean into the fear that will soften your heart.

You are here to change people, but the alchemy is in your softness.

Fuck the world.

Show them your wounds and let them heal.

Trusting that your wounding has no purpose.

They are road maps to the places the world couldn't accept in themselves.

Show them a new way.

Until Then

Tell me to love you.

Reach for me.

Ask me to stay.

Take my hands

and my mouth.

Put your heart against mine.

Breathe my breath.

Capture my gaze. Don't look away.

Pick me.

Choose me.

Love me.

Until then, I belong to the temple in my mind.

My heart beats for Lakshmi.

My breath.

My heartbeat.

My love.

Escape

Today I had to choose my shadow.

To honor this pain beneath my ribs.

This ache that has been begging for my attention all weekend.

He asks for some affection, some time, some tenderness.

Yet, I pushed through.

I went dancing, and through my hips I wanted to cry.

So I had a drink.

Then I noticed I began to leave my body.

So I escaped home to sleep.

The desire to touch myself sounded paltry.

It would be too real.

This morning I woke up, deciding to meditate in ritual for hours.

Not realizing that too was an escape.

I yearned to leave.

As I got myself lost, my heart opened.

I miss my mom.

I miss my teacher.

I miss my life being easy.

As the tears burned my eyes, grateful that I no longer give a fuck about hiding my face, the sky too began to cry.

Clouds came to comfort me, cold rain soothes my too tender skin, and the wind.

The sharp and cutting wind, clearing away the old,

ripples through my body, forcing me to feel again.

Making room for the future and my joy.

Rising

Is it because I'm part Gemini?

My triumphs always tinged with the

eyes of my demons.
Feeling powerful, worthy, joyful.
Then turn to a manic hunger.
To be loved, kissed, used and toyed with.
I ignore this whoreish gnawing.

Ashamed it stills runs through my veins.
How do I heal this hole?
The one my sister has. And my small town.
Convinced that only a man can make my heart race,
edging passion and worth.
My reward being tossed aside

like a glove in the desert.
Waiting for him to change.
To wake up and adore me.
To choose me.
As the face of my lover turns into the face of my father-
I finally see.
He doesn't know how.

He cannot handle another drop.
I see the laughable picture.
A regal Queen that holds herself captive, convinced her
desires are doomed.

Locked away in safety, longing for a life so sexy she can't help but pour over.

Seeing the stars through a dusty window that she refuses to clean.

Telling herself that the sun can only do harm to her delicate skin.

Running naked through her kingdom would send her wild soul soaring.

A sensation so innocent and pure, she'd surely die in the moment.

Forgive Me

I can no longer afford to carry my failures.
I let go.
I forgive myself.
I gave the most I was capable of.
I did the best I could.
I allow every moment to be fresh and new.
I am willing to be great.
I am willing to release any person, pattern or place that
is not for my greatness.
I am responsible for this moment.
It's brand new.

A Vow

You are talented, vibrant, fierce and soft.
God placed you here knowing your purpose is big.
As big as your smile.
As determined as your walk.
Sharp and witty, with a huge heart.
You were not born to walk the beaten path.
You are a story teller, a priestess, Durga herself.
You love deeply and fiercely.
When you speak, angels nod along.
When you dance, the wind picks up its pace.
When you laugh, even pain takes pause.
My vow to you is to choose Love.
To hold you in the dark.
To appreciate your softness, even when you're rigid.
To embrace your darkness, because God gave it to you,
then gave you to the world.
I will honor your body.
Every meal will be an offering.
Every bath, a ritual.
Every kiss, a mediation.
And every breath, a prayer.
I will tell you everyday how precious you are.
I will seek new ways to feed your soul
and expand your joy.
I will never abandon you.
I will remind you every moment how much I love you.

Self Portrait

I love this woman.

Look at her scars.

Can you see her sadness?

I know you feel her. It's impossible not to.

Her tears are hot, her love is big.

She is the universe. She is human. She saved me, again.

Woman and Me

I am reckless.

A know it all.

When I make mistakes I may put my head in the sand.

I'm prone to depression, anxiety

and Godiva truffles.

I cry for day dreams and dream of failing.

I can be sharp. Guarded.

I project my emotions onto loved ones.

I play the victim.

I make messes, sometimes I leave them.

I'm not the best listener.

I fall in love with potential.

I'm obsessive, controlling, introverted.

I think I know best.

I'm afraid of depending on others.

Terrified of power.

I'm often mean to myself.

And yet- I'm magic.

I'm a full person.

So ready and worthy. Just as I am.

So ready and worthy. Just as I am.

Artemis

Beneath the pain and tightness is a slow,

grinning smile.
I came for change.
We see struggle and fear,

She sees the perfect opportunity.
My body may appear delicate,

soft and built for a mans hands.
It's my vehicle to power,

through freedom and persistence.
Take my youth, take my books, my words and my breasts.
But you know that I am here for change,

and the time is now.

Cheeky

I am too much.
I am so loud.
I am hard to get to.
I'm really good at pushing you away.
My dreams- Huge. Wild. Important.

Beloved

The things that have happened are gone.

You don't have to identify with

"Poor Amy" or "Typical Amy".

You are allowed to be who you really are,

not a reaction to your past.

Yes, you've been raped.

Yes, you've been abandoned.

Yes, you've been sabotaged, beaten, isolated and left

disparaged.

You are meant to be successful.

Surrounded by people you love and trust.

You can have an exciting and fulfilling life.

Being a martyr doesn't make you a good woman.

Live your life.

Do what excites you.

You are not your past.

You have permission to be

who you are supposed to be.

I Dream of A King

I'm ready.
For you.

My body tingles with your nearness.
My excitement is slow and grinning.

Your legacy needs you, but you need me.

I am not your queen, but I am divine.

I am the goddess, anointing your crown.
Steadying your journey and kissing your cheek.

I am ready for you to walk through the door.

I've left it open.

She Speaks

When you speak, we speak.

I know you're lost.

We're lost together.

Sister I feel your anger at God.

In all fairness, he didn't promise easy.

You can listen to your heart, which I know you hear.

I hear your heart too.

There's another voice, telling you to be patient. Telling
you to ground and maybe settle for a while.

By the quiver of your chin, I know that you're not built
for settling.

So, why not?

Why not go all in?

Risk it all.

When you speak, we speak.

When you live, we live.

Why not live your purpose for me, for your sisters, for
the people that need your offering.

When you speak, we speak.

What would you like to hear?

Her

I'm never upset for the reasons I think.
I'm healing, I know.
I feel it in the burning under my eyes.
A quiver in my chest.
A hollowness between my legs.
I crave attention, text messages, kisses, comfort.

Security.
I miss a man that doesn't exist.
A band aid for my holes.
There was a man on Tuesday, he made no promises.
He pulled my hair, but wouldn't look me in the eye.
I did catch him staring.
His attention warmed my heart.
Again, he made no promises.
My imagination can be mean,
a deprecating monster.
I pine for him, even just a fraction.
To know that he's not inside a woman, a model, a god-
dess.
Looking into her eyes, telling her everything I long to
hear.

Universal

I see your soul in everything
Or is it just my mind?
Comforted by my delusions.
You keep pulling me into the past, until it's all I see.
Remember in Ancient Rome, you couldn't keep your
hands clean.
Your mouth always found my neck,
Until my husband had your head.
In Paris, I was your favorite whore.
A softness in my face.
You couldn't decide to raise me or use me.

It was both.
My favorite is America.
Revolution on our breath.
Secrets were our game.
I held you to my breast and wept,
knowing you belonged to your country.
We met again, a truer version.
The only thing keeping us apart
is the fear of love.
I'm not sure we belong.
I love it in your arms,
Until the past is all I see.

Only If

My loneliness is too precious to give away.

Even though I crave a tender touch,

it must be tantric.

I long for tender kisses along my neck,

but only if they're golden.

The way my blood flows reminds me that I want to be

filled,

but only if it's sacred.

I won't give up my pity party unless he is a king.

A divine being in my path,

aligned for my entire being.

So I cry and I curl on my side,

cherishing my tears.

Knowing that he's coming, he's magic and he's real.

Bedhead

In my sleep I dreamt about a warrior.

Not a hero, not a sadist, but a man.

Aggression is underrated.

Not good or bad,

just a driving force of presence that has been

apologized for or shamed.

My soul automatically recognizes.

I'm no longer looking for potential.

Warrior or bust.

Tribal

I see a little girl that was rejected.

I pick her up, I hold her in my arms and

whisper into her blonde hair

"I've got you. I love you."

My walls served no one.

I no longer need to fortify and protect.

I am safe. I am love.

Love Without Condition

You don't agree with me.

You won't see me.

Your lips won't touch mine.

It's never on my time.

You don't know where I've been.

I want to hold your hand.

Can you see my beauty?

I polished it for you. I hid my darkness for you.

My Jezebel, my harlot, my queen of Sheba.

I didn't think you wanted us, so I locked them in my tissues.

The key is hidden in my breathless smile.

My shifty eyes.

My people pleasing guile.

And yet you hate me.

Just like he did.

You're all the same.

I know it's hate when you never call.

I know it's hate when I stumble.

I know it's hate when I eat alone.

But I'll get in a cab. I'll come running when you text.

I'll sneak a sexy message, dripping with desperation.

Come inside, I don't need protection.

Come inside, it's connection.

If I give you everything you'll want me.

A late night rejection.

Manchild

Why you? What is it?

I hear the insecurity in your voice.

The unsurety of your purpose.

Which gets me wet.

There's a deeper quiet that awakens my soul,

bringing her to the surface.

You're not from a past life,

I've never come this far.

In my immaturity I crave attachment, indulgence.

Convincing myself that life is feeding my hunger.

You are a child and an old man.

I cannot read you.

The mystery drawing me in, the tenderness getting me
hooked, your hesitation driving me mad.

I am both sated and gaping.

Your body peeling the makeshift patches off my rotten
wounds.

The most beautiful I have ever been, with a smell so
rancid I cringe.

Dripping with desire, we slide so easily together.

Except a piercing burn of fear amplifies my sensation.

I never want that again, except everyday.

Cord Cutting

I will pray for you.

I always do.

I send you light, straight into your heart.

Waking you up, healing your wounds and giving you road maps to your deepest desires.

I released you before.

The moon guided me to call back my hooks in you.

I shivered in confusion as they dissolved into the ocean.

Trusting my moon, trusting my voice and the whispers of freedom.

Sex gave us an intimacy that we didn't earn.

I want to be your friend, not your lover.

If there's no starting over, I understand.

Thank you for the lessons, thank you for the warmth and thank you for healing that part of me that didn't know better.

Gods

Hell is pretending I'm a human again.

Ripples control my spine.

Serpentine beats escape my hips at the dinner table.

My smile is not for this moment.

My tears are from another life.

Move in me again, Oh Lord.

I'm not healed.

Touch me in your way.

I still want to cry.

Take me higher again,

I'm not ready to come back.

Deep, Red and Sacred

Dancing with you is my favorite, we always draw a crowd.

My hips and your smile know no strangers.

Tonight I crave you, running my hands over your strong chest.
Your t shirt teases me, driving me wild.

If I took it off now, you wouldn't mind.

But I can't wait to put my mouth on you.

Feel your heart beat against my bare breasts.

Lock eyes with you and forget time.
I can't wait for you to sweat on me. Drip on me. Slide against me and into me.
I completely surrender to you and God. My body is your temple. Your body is my shrine.

I've never slept so deeply than beside you, having your body close to mine.

The comfort of your skin tracing my curves.
I am so grateful for you. My soul feels at ease when you're around. My heart is full. My pussy pulsing.
I'm so glad our love is lit.

It's deep, it's red and it's sacred.

Isabel

I see a queen.

Regal, warm, powerful.

Playful when possible, sturdy on the path.

Realizing the importance of her health and happiness.

The balance it takes to lead and shift dimensions.

The fear that comes with new gifts.

The understanding that growth is not comfortable

but rewarding.

That acting in fear sinks ships.

My higher self is warm, funny, loves to dance.

She loves her momma and her skin.

She's tuned in, turned on and turned up.

Always ready, always listening.

I want to be a woman of outrageous joy.

I want to be a woman of divine courage.

She sees herself in every person.

My enemy does not exist.

Because she is who needs healing.

She's an incredible business owner.

A divine mother.

Protector. Purveyor of consciousness.

Activator of wisdom.

Forever loving.

Forever guiding.

Forever protecting.

She loves to fall in love.

Everyday she falls deeper.

Flesh and Spirit

There's no such thing as closure.
I know you can't give me the intimacy I'm looking for.
I do love you.
You gave me a new depth in love.
I miss the way you'd linger and softly touch me.
I still tingle where you kissed my hair.
I let my tears fall for these tender moments.
Not lost, but fleeting.
An anchor into a higher love.
As I'm propelled into more unknown, I can't help but
ache for the next time I see you on the street.
Letting my longing reach out to you for a moment,

telling you I still care.
Knowing I should step back and let you unfold.
As much as I love to watch you, I'm not your angel.
I am meant to be a catalyst to your great love.
My instructions are to walk away and wish you well.
Sometimes when I pray, I see your naked chest.
Pulling me back into those moments of flesh and spirit.
Seeing you happy turns me on.
Whoever gets to kiss you next- I bless them.
Not to tie myself to you, but to know that your

pleasure keeps going.

It's You

If I wasn't paying attention, I would have missed it.
I would have chosen the one that fed my wounds.
I would have ignored your smile and begged for him to
see me.
I would have cried myself to sleep,

hoping he'd call tomorrow.
I would search the past for a glimpse of hope.
Feeding the rejection, the pain, the voice that says

"It's you. You're too much."
Thank God I stopped to breathe.
Recognized your voice and your need to say my name.
The way you understand my stubbornness.
The way you stare at my mouth, trying to catch the
words and the silence.
I can't say your name yet, but I'm working on it.
It's Shiva for now.
Or Kismet.
Forever connected by breath and the moon.
You touch me when I'm sleeping.
My astral lover.
Projecting the future into visions.
Our fights,
Our passion,
Our joy.

I promise not to future trip and miss these moments.
The first time you acknowledge me from our night time
visits.
The first time you miss me.
The first time you ask for more.

Fairy Tales

You asked me how I shift my fears.

Waking up next to you, I knew.

You are here to show me the illusion.

How limitless our passion is and how my body keeps up.

How money keeps flowing in– even if I'm not paying attention.

How the love I've always wanted has wolf eyes, angel wings and is singing in my shower.

So yes, I believe in fairy tales.

Stories of faith.

When heavenly creatures come to Earth and transform into kings.

Helping me to remember my divinity.

My kingdom in heaven.

My immense power and beauty.

The power that runs through my words.

I believe it finally,

Only love exists.

Touch

I'm drenched.

And you haven't touched me yet.

My back arches when you bite your lip.

My thighs shake at the sight of your tongue.

My breath deepens and my breasts reach for your hands.

My mouth waters and my tongue searches for your skin.

My hips are trembling for your hands.

My shoulders begging for your teeth.

The thought of your mouth on my neck erases any thought.

Only the moan that escapes my lips as I grind in my empty sheets.

Kiss me, bite me, lick me, spank me-

I'm dying.

Smell me, taste me, watch me, hear me-

Touch me already.

Rise

Everything's different now.

I bow to you.

You bathe me.

I can't wait to share a new form of prayer.

To have a man so divine, able to hold my love.

Able to set me free while holding me close.

My past creeps up from time to time.

Terrified that my darkness will ruin you or turn you
away.

But knowing that God gave me you.

There's a reason, there's a purpose.

My love is just getting started.

I cried today thinking about you.

That's how perfect you are.

To appreciate myself on a deeper level.

I'm the kind of woman that attracts you.

Pure. Powerful. Funny. Smart. Driven. Loving. Sexy, complete.

Your smile, your pleasure, your enthusiasm.

I don't burn for you.

I burn to become you. To rise in love.

Scry

Even in my fear, I can smile.

I was ready for you.

You are worth stepping over fear, walking through fire.

Here I am, burning.

Being refined and cleansed so that I can fully receive you.

I constantly pray to let you go.

Knowing it's the only way to walk beside you.

It's the only way to step into myself.

The woman I am came to this plane to burn, to soothe, to protect.

Your soul gave me a staircase of stars.

Giving me a higher perspective.

Skipping over thorns and muddy paths.

Maybe I was kind to you in a past life.

Maybe your soul took pity.

Or maybe you saw the divine potential of love in me.

Giving me glimpses of you.

Asking me to choose you through the masks of ego and the veils of incomplete love.

A wiser woman lives in my womb.

Her voice quietly breaking attachments to magicians and heroes.

When your face appeared, it wasn't easy to accept.

But loving you has been a memory in my cells.

I'm awake, alive, full of breath.

To stare into your eyes 6,000 miles away has been the most intense lovemaking.

To hear your deep voice as I sleep is the sweetest grace.

You melt the past.

You have my future.

The only choice is surrender.

Sorry

You said it today.

I knew it would happen.

And I'm sorry.

I don't feel the same way.

I can't, the universe won't let me.

I don't want to disappoint you, but I don't miss you.

There's no way.

You're always with me.

When I'm overwhelmed, I feel your breath in my lungs.

When I'm alone, your heart pours into mine.

When I can't keep going, I hear your timbering accent in my bones say "G'Day Gorgeous. You're made for this."

This morning I woke up on your broad chest, curled into your long body.

My fingers running through your hair.

I don't miss you,

You haven't left.

Vision

I ran out of words.

I used them all, wishing for you.

My list was lengthy and specific.

My research kept me up late at night.

Pages and pages of desire and longing.

I knew that when you came I would have so much to say.

Except all the words have gone.

I see glimpses of them on your skin.

Unable to write any longer, all I can do is breathe.

The more I relax into you, the less I have to say.

It's a feeling of life.

It's the sound of joy.

It's the taste of my tongue, dancing against my palette.

The smell of my sweat, cooling on my skin.

And the vision of your face, softening in front of mine, longing to be kissed.

Dragons

Why use words when I can set the world on fire?

Let my roar be a warning to the flames.

Born out of disempowerment and gaping wounds.

Torching any bridges over calm waters.

Destroying and barricading myself in fire.

I would leave my burning at times, pretending the smoke between my teeth wasn't painful.

Eventually running back to the red embers of my prison.

Until you.

My eyes like lasers,

Tracking my beloved.

My smile, an inviting gate.

Filling my belly with air, adding the fuel of purpose-

And you.

The spark in my chest.

Neither good nor bad, but clean.

I spit flames of courage, eternal love and power.

Creating a ring of warmth to draw you in.

Ready to ignite the world in a ceremony so brilliant my

ancestors weep.

Keep my fire, beloved.

It's for you.

Smile into my hearth.

Cry over the beauty.

Sway to the crackling of my soul.

I'll set the world on fire-

And you.

You'll build a new world from the ashes.

Twin

I hold the vision with you, my love.

Standing beside you,

Bathing all who need it in unconditional love.

Feeling you hold my hand, even when you're not beside me.

There's just something about us.

I'll set the world on fire.

You'll calm them.

God will move them.

Everything

You flew 6,428 miles to kiss me.

I was terrified.

The idea of you scared me.

The man that came in from China didn't.

He was gentle, patient, strong and fun as hell.

You went along with my crazy ideas.

Made every moment sacred.

You're so much more than the outline of a man I used to think about before bed.

You're everything.

Away

I want to take you with me, so I do.

When I see a beautiful tree, in my mind I whisper and point, "Look babe, it's for us."

A stranger smiles and warms my heart, I smile back at you.

Every time I hear my own laugh, it echoes your booming voice.

When I want to cry, I let you kiss my tears.

As I tremble, I feel your warm hands on my body.

I fall asleep at night, I curl into your body, whispering into your chest:

"Thank you for everything."

You

I trust you.

I love you.

I need you.

I want you.

I got you.

I respect you.

I recognize you.

I feel you.

I miss you.

I have you.

I breathe you.

I speak you.

I hear you.

I taste you.

I cradle you.

I call you.

I receive you.

I beckon you.

I tease you.

I push you.

I edge you.

I indulge you.

I spoil you.

I pick you.

I choose you.

I touch you.

I mirror you.

I adore you.

I need you.

China

My mouth is watering.

My lips are soft.

Searching, restless, heated.

I'm on my way.

Masks and Men

It's not you.

It's God moving through you.

Kissing me, wanting to be with me.

I see a billion stars when I look at you, other dimensions
I cannot touch.

But they touch me with your hands.

Smile at me with such amazing tenderness.

I feel myriads behind your words.

Whispering ancient secrets in my sensitive ears.

I see God in your face, love in your eyes and feel the
earth in your strength.

A lucky girl am I.

The divine mortalized to walk with me, to smile.

Not a man, but a vessel.

So the universe could experience me.

Fine

I was fine.

Until I prayed for more.

My quietly exciting life looked shiny and full.

I didn't realize how dull my heart beat sounded.

How clenched my shoulders became,

How they curled forward to protect my heart.

I was fine.

Until you kissed me.

Breaking my heart and birthing a tender one.

It beats your name, aches from stretching each day and longs to rest in you.

Not fine. Not pretending.

My warrior of love, pacing the floors for your other half.

Fighting and pulling me in, feeling me and waiting with a naughty smile.

Anticipating the moment you get to destroy my illusions.

Removing words like "dull", "weak", "comfortable" and "fine".

I'll never be fine again.

Longing

There's a new longing that I have.

A "Wouldn't it be nice if he were beside me..."

It lives between my breasts, but it started in my hips.

Sometimes it travels,

Seeing glimpses between my brows.

For now I'm hungry and a little sad.

I know he's coming,

He's definitely real.

For an impatient woman, it's a new heartbreak each day.

Not that she's doomed.

But that she may not be ready.

Stay

If you get here.

When you get here.

What if you leave,

And I end up going with you?

When you pack your suitcase,

It's full of my blood.

When you hail a cab,

Its my laughter sitting beside you.

My happiness curled around your neck.

And my peace tucked into your pocket.

I know what I'm supposed to be.

Fortified, brave, forgiving.

But I can't forgive my heart.

She's bold on her own, but longing to be held.

I'm scared to open the door.

Knowing it'll be the greatest love of my life.

What if you leave and I fall apart?

Is it better to have lost?

If you get here.

When you get here.

Do me a favor, please?

Stay.

Dreamer

I hope that you never ever, for even the flap of a birds wing,

Stop feeling my complete adoration for you.

Even in my weakness,

My exhaustion,

My heaviness– I never stop seeing you.

I may hear old voices telling me I don't deserve you or that it's too much or too hard,

But you're never dim or unworthy.

You're the brightest light.

The wildest tongue and the softest love.

My job is to remember so I can show up as the woman that knows she deserves you.

Royal

I miss you already.

My hips opening for your heart.

My heart stretching for your throne.

Sit beside mine, my king.

I leave my doors unlocked, windows thrown open.

Let it rain.

Let the wind clear my madness.

A little earth on my sheets.

Ether of my dreams.

Fire in my brow.

I'm a soldier, a mother and a crow.

But you don't care.

I love that you don't care.

Mama

You died before I got to tell you.

I'm angry.

It wasn't enough.

It wasn't real.

It hurt.

I'm sad.

I should have brought more flowers.

I should have cried more.

I should have called you back.

I'm scared.

What if I end up like you?

What if my kids look like you?

What if I forget to live, like you?

I'm sorry.

I'm no longer a child.

I am beautiful.

I want to let you in.

Death never scared me.

Hospitals don't make me sorry.

It's the little girl curled around her momma's leg that haunts me.

I thought you were beautiful.

I loved your crazy.

I miss your voice.

Forgive yourself, then forgive me.

Maybe I had to wait.

Distance of death finally bringing us closer.

I want to be good, momma.

I want to live.

Misery

Get away from me.

I'm comfortable in my prison.

Stop staring at me with those eyes.

There's no hiding and I'm not ready.

Don't say my name.

It breaks my heart and gives me hope.

I'd like to stay the same.

Quite telling me you love me.

There's no room,

I only have space for my baggage.

Stop smiling at me like the sun.

I was planning on staying in the shadows, shivering in my loneliness.

If only you'd stop loving me.

So I could stay so miserable.

She Awaits

She doesn't search, she knows you're coming.

You've been summoned.

A warrior and a muse, let your hair down.

She likes you wild.

Let your feet kiss the ground to her chambers.

Use your breath for strength.

She knows your eyes, they belong to her.

Do not hold back, she will touch your skin.

A caress unbearable to the weak.

Do not speak, she doesn't need words.

She wants to meet your soul.

Your lips will burn,

Your belly will hunger.

Do not rush, you will not be disappointed.

She's here for the pleasure of God.

Leave now, letting go of calculations and agendas.

Do not hesitate.

You've been summoned by your Goddess.

She awaits.

My Goddess

And there she was.

Not the ocean,

Not my angel,

But myself.

Staring into my deep eyes with lightning and fire rippling through her hair.

A goddess so beautiful, I couldn't help but love her deeply.

She raised her hand to my belly and asked "Are you ready?"

As her ethereal hands turned into blades of obsidian,

She plunged them into my belly.

My ears pounded with the sound of wind, painful memories and my distractions.

"Focus." she warned.

As I concentrated on the pain, it melted.

I could feel a deep pulsing.

Pulling all the darkness from my toes, my brow, through my heart, gathering and solidifying in my belly.

She then pulled the dark orb out of my body.

Letting it breathe a moment before disappearing in a flash of light.

I could feel a hole,

A fresh and tender space.

My Goddess kissed me.

Filling my body with pure light,

Begging me to live fully.

Light Worker

There's a deep peace in me.

A mother that keeps me still amidst the chaos of my birth.

I've found her in angels, in music and in art.

Today she's the cozy wool socks as I watch the snow fall.

Reminding me that my mistakes were from not listening.

From disconnecting and leaving this body I signed.

That I am not my own to judge.

That there is much movement on the other side so I may stay in joy.

Because the experiences I hold are not wisdom, they are not lessons-

They are barriers to my heart and to the power I am.

Feeling the buzz of gratitude,

I am shocked at my ignorance.

For my wings are made of light, my hands of obsidian, and love-

Love is written on my forehead.

Deep Space

"What does it feel like?" he asks.

Like heaven and hell.

I'm dying, but it's all I ever wanted.

A place I remember, but have never been.

I have no name; no voice.

I am endless for those moments.

Full of God and of wisdom.

Then the truths fade away and I am vacuumed back into my body.

Breathing helps.

Lover

I'm not ashamed of my happiness.

Dripping with love.

Fiery in purpose.

Strong in flow.

And looking at me with wolf eyes.

Him

I want to hate him, but I don't.

I don't deserve to be in fear.

I don't deserve to be quiet.

I don't deserve to be hit.

How do I father myself?

Take your power back, everyday.

You feel, even when it's hard.

And you love.

Courage and all.

Wild Orange

I miss him.

Not because I'm weak or hungry.

But because I feel him without touching his skin.

A pull in my heart, a sound in my peripheral vision.

He's uncomfortable.

The hardest part of a connection so deep is standing
still when the lessons come.

But the joy.

The joy is overwhelming.

When he laughs I am filled with that pure, wild orange.

Mornings

Woman, never change yourself.

I need you.

Let the labels fall off, let your favorite things change;

Let your morning coffee become tea then become milk.

There was never a perfect answer.

You are my answer. I need you.

Change your patterns, change the road, change the
window you dream out of-

But never change who you are.

Become nothing but more of you, because that is what
I need.

Bankrupt

My freedom doesn't look like yours,

Stop trying to compare.

My path was built with me in mind and strength that
got me there.

I was lead through the darkness,

And as I come out the other side,

I cannot waste my love or light listening to your time.

I forgive you for wanting things to go your way,

And I forgive myself for caring.

But the hour has come to piss you off

And be joyful in my daring.

You may not understand my freedom,

And I don't get your motives.

But the day has come and I am done

Weighing on my shoulders.

Admitting defeat and failure,

Kept me from my ease.

So now I yell my failures out, smile,

and go as I please.

One day we might meet again and I'll feel a tinge of sorrow.

But it's better than the hole I felt,

avoiding all tomorrows.

Manifest

And here you are.

A testament to the skins I've shed and the light I've touched.

Here you are.

The smile that starts in my thighs.

Here you are.

The king I've always worshipped.

The voice of love in my dreams.

The man I didn't know exists.

And here you are.

Just a human, just as longing, just as real.

Gypsy

It's true.

All of it.

And now you know my secrets,

I'm going to cast my spell.

I'm calling in outrageous joy.

Whispering to desire to join the party.

Asking fire to burn through anxious clouds.

Crying out to the earth to keep my feet bound.

Light a candle,

Look into my eyes,

Repeat after me,

Let me in.

Sometimes

Sometimes I take you for granted.

Sometimes I'm exhausted from all the learning and growing we do.

Sometimes I'm a bully.

Sometimes I love to project my problems onto you.

Blaming my sweet lover for anything that doesn't go my way.

With all the heartache of sometimes, I never stop feeling your love.

I never stop having fun with you.

And I never forget what a lucky woman I am.

Breathe

Can you love yourself through it?

When ancient shame bubbles up in your belly to cut off your voice.

When a shrill tendril commands to manipulate and control, or just accept the violation.

When your inner child is throwing a fit, she's cold and hungry.

Can I find my way back to love?

Can I sit still in the icy river?

Can I keep walking as my heart bursts into flames in the desert?

Blind to the nights sky, can I trust my heart?

Can I embrace the good?

Can I stop clinging to the rocks of childhood, to float in a sea of my own creation?

I'd love to say yes.

I'd love to pretend that I have surety.

I'd love to comfort you.

I'd love to put this storm to rest.

In this moment I can only promise to breathe.

Priestess

I've travelled a long way.

It's time to honor the timing of my life.

I've been known to pull things into existence, to force and shoulder the things I want.

My higher self only cares that I'm honoring my soul.

Surrendering to it.

Letting go of control.

Today I forgive myself for being cruel, for rushing, for acting out of fear, for hiding, for dominating and manipulating.

I forgive myself for this life and lives past.

For me, my family, my relationships, our ancestors and their relationships through all time and lives...

Please help us love and bless each other;

Bless ourselves.

Be at peace now and forever.

Please and thank you.

Smoke and Shame

If you're in it for the fame or fortune, prepare to be humbled.

This work is about seeing yourself for the first time.

All the ugly.

All the shadow.

And having the compassion for yourself to keep going.

Note To Self

Be aware of the place in you that sometimes misses the

point.

She lets fear guide her into overthinking.

Like throwing pearls on a pile of trash,

Praying that it keeps her warm and makes her famous.

She talks too fast and explains away her inner knowing.

She is smart, so you have to use your heart.

Steady On

You never did anything wrong.

You just needed time to find your why.

In every moment remember:

I am god.

I am safe.

I am successful.

See how your decisions change, your body, your breath, your smile.

Let your soul live.

Dance in between your masculine and feminine.

Cherish the time you came into the world,

Cherish your parents, your lessons, and the deep love you are able to feel.

You are well equipped to live an incredible life.

Sandy

I don't love that way anymore.

It started off innocent and shy.

After puberty she was bold and daring.

The next was hollow and dangerous.

What she thought was love became an act of survival.

It got a little better.

Love became fun again, for a little while.

Except it didn't feel good.

So she shrunk herself down, bought a new role.

Sickeningly sweet and moldy,

love felt stale and pointless.

So she ran.

She chose to unlove.

As she unraveled, losing her mind-

She lost years of pain and heartache.

Life became colorful again.

Love, still scary. But life, amazing.

Food tasted amazing.

Her body blossomed like a flower.

She smiled with all of her teeth,

danced with her entire body.

Looking in the mirror a privilege,

bathing became a ritual.

One day while watching the clouds,

She realized this is love.

And thus began her love affair.

Kings came and went.

Soulmates flooded her streets.

And again, a little voice whispers :"He's coming."

Unlike the love she's had with men,

but more like the sun.

It'll leave her nourished, warm and content.

Just like the sunlight, she never has to search.

She just waits until morning.